THE OCEAN WORLD COLORING BOOK

Reveal the beauty of the seas

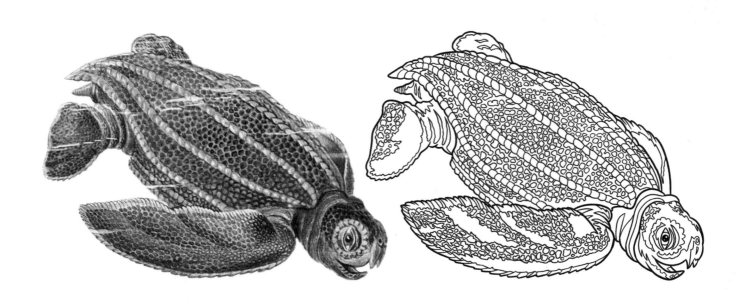

SIRIUS

SIRIUS

This edition published in 2024 by Sirius Publishing, a division of
Arcturus Publishing Limited,
26/27 Bickels Yard, 151–153 Bermondsey Street,
London SE1 3HA

ISBN: 978-1-3988-4487-2
CH01122NT

Printed in China

THE OCEAN WORLD COLORING BOOK

Introduction

Although the world's oceans still remain something of a mystery, and marine biologists continue to explore the seabeds, discovering new species of flora and fauna, there is much to marvel at beneath the waves.

This delightful coloring book contains a set of images specially selected from some of the earliest illustrated books published on the natural history of the oceans, including *The Great Barrier Reef of Australia: its products and potentialities* by William Saville-Kent, *Les délices des yeux et de l'esprit, ou, Collection générale differentes espèces de coquillages que la mer renferme* by Georg Wolfgang Knorr, *Kunst formen der Natur.* by Professor Dr Ernst Haeckel, *The Naturalist's Miscellany* by George Shaw et al, *Ocean Gardens* by H. Noel Humphreys, and *Thesaurus conchyliorum* by G. B. Sowerby.

The original images offer you the opportunity to follow the actual color combinations of the subjects depicted, but alternatively, feel free to create your own color scheme. All you need to do is collect your coloring pencils or markers together, find somewhere to sit and relax, and enjoy the beauties of the sealife that lies within these pages.

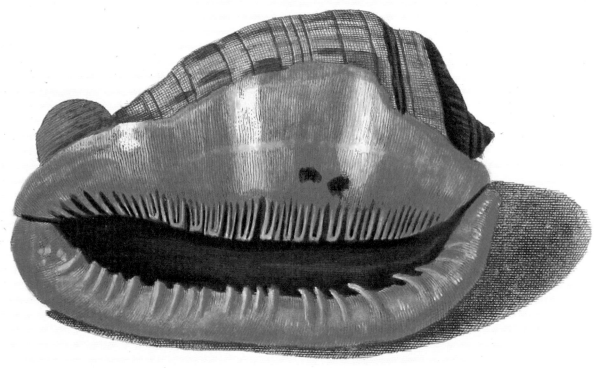

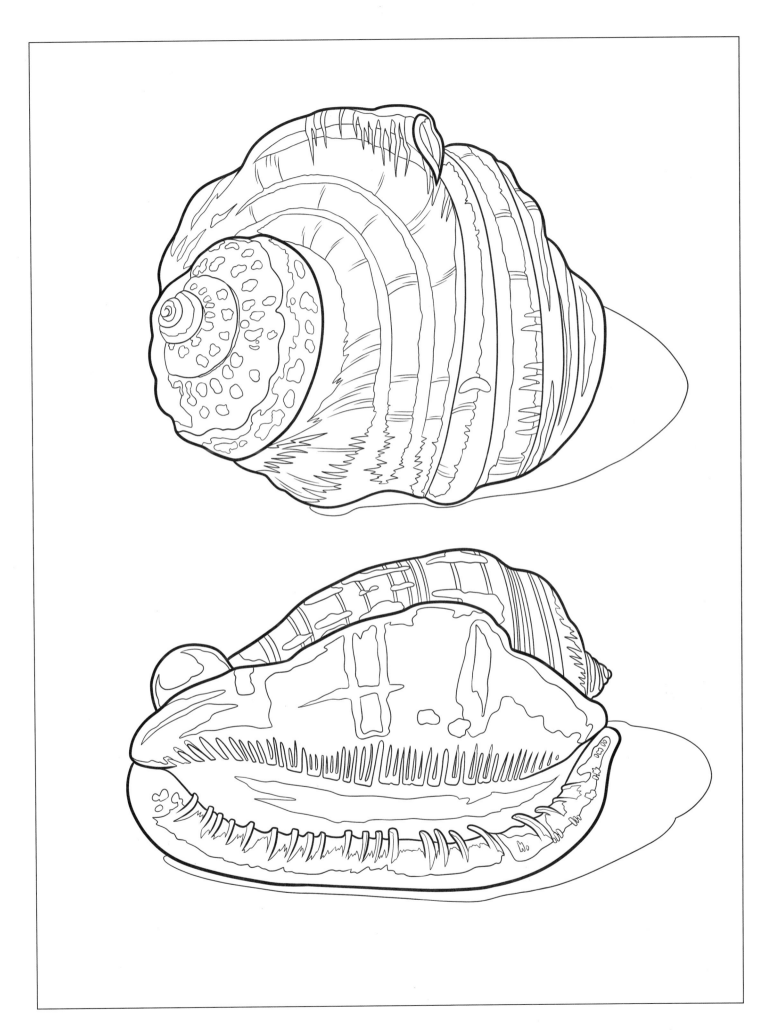

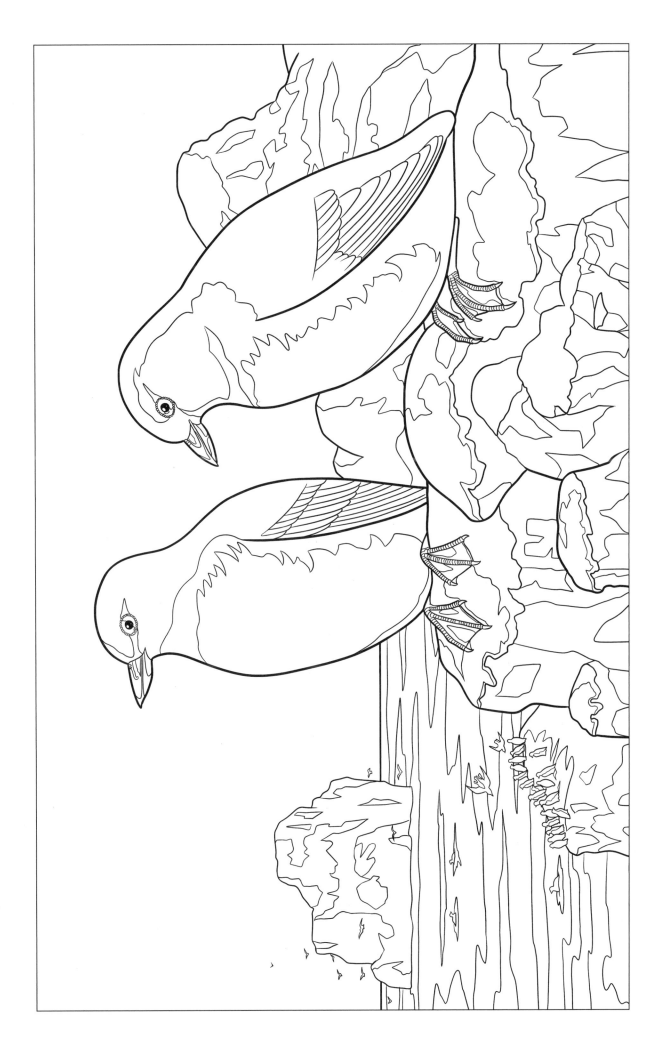

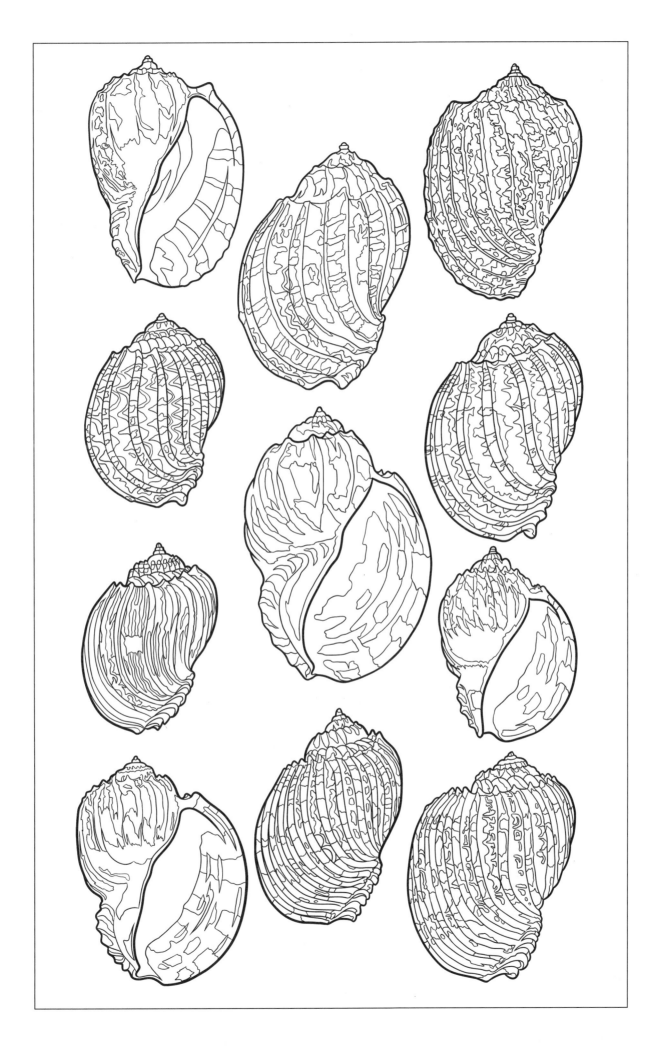

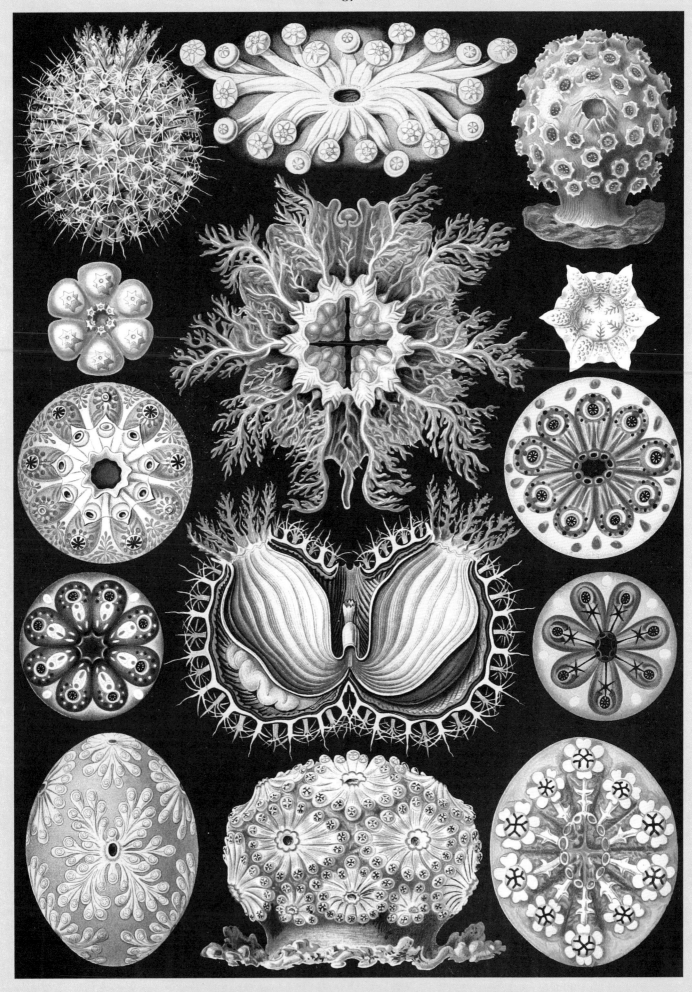

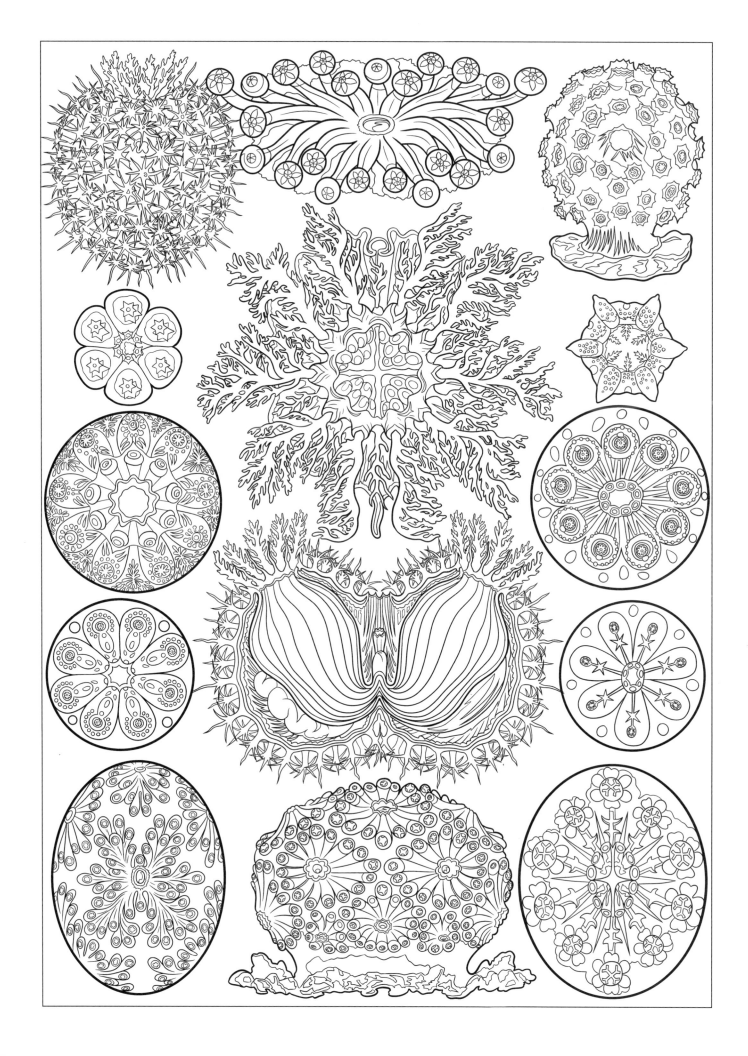

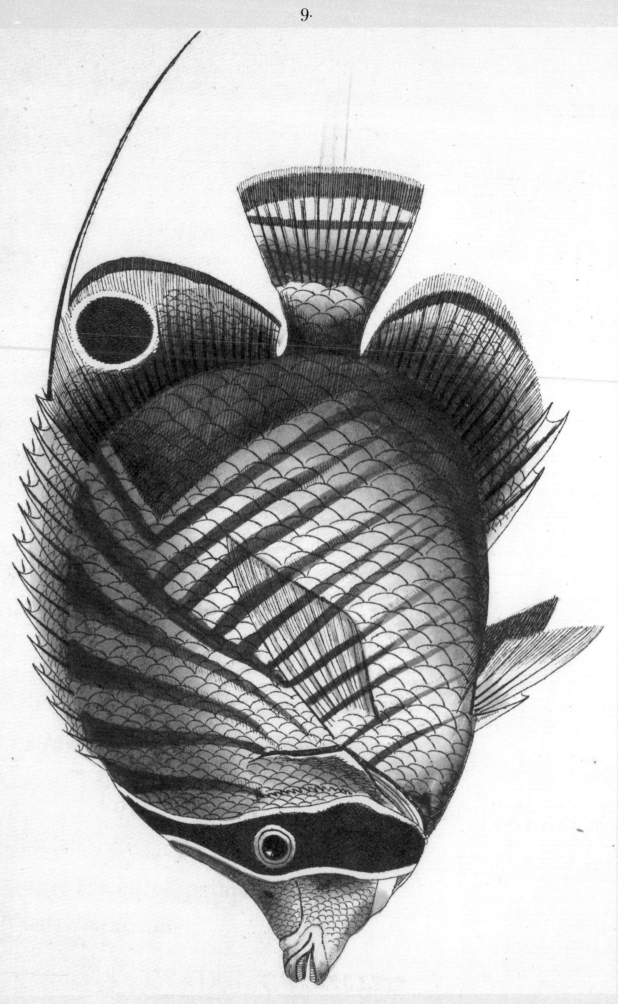

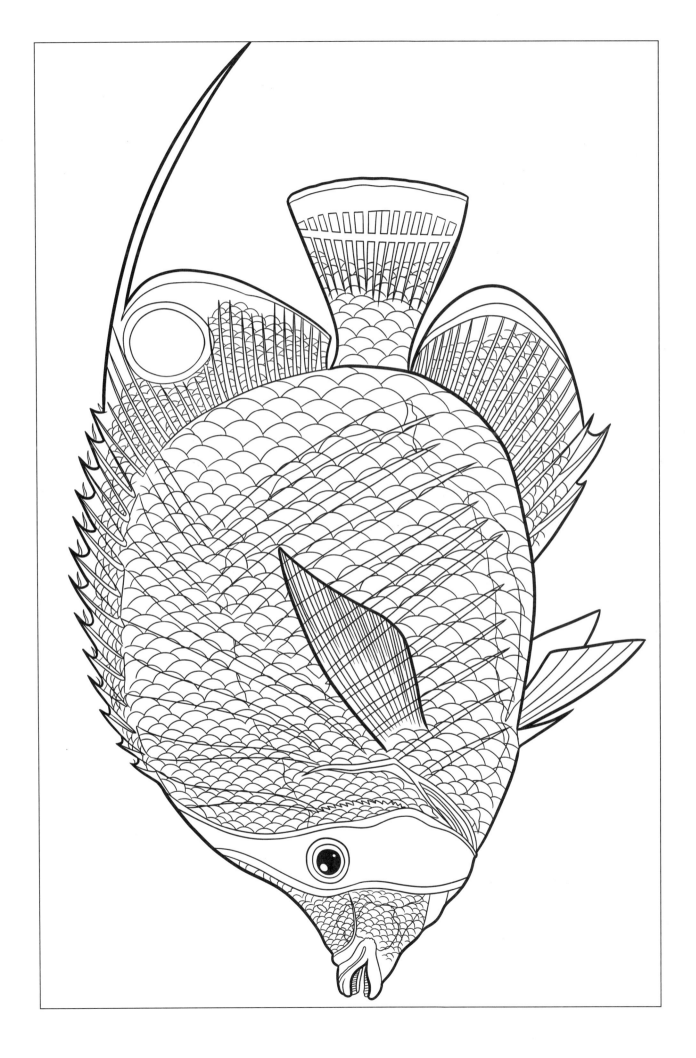

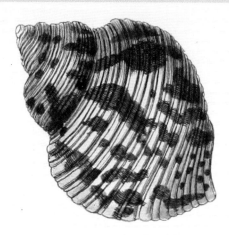

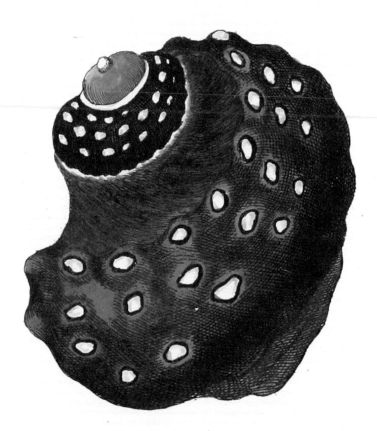

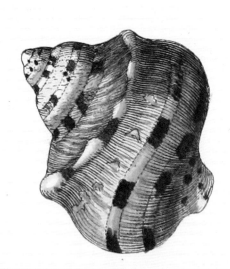

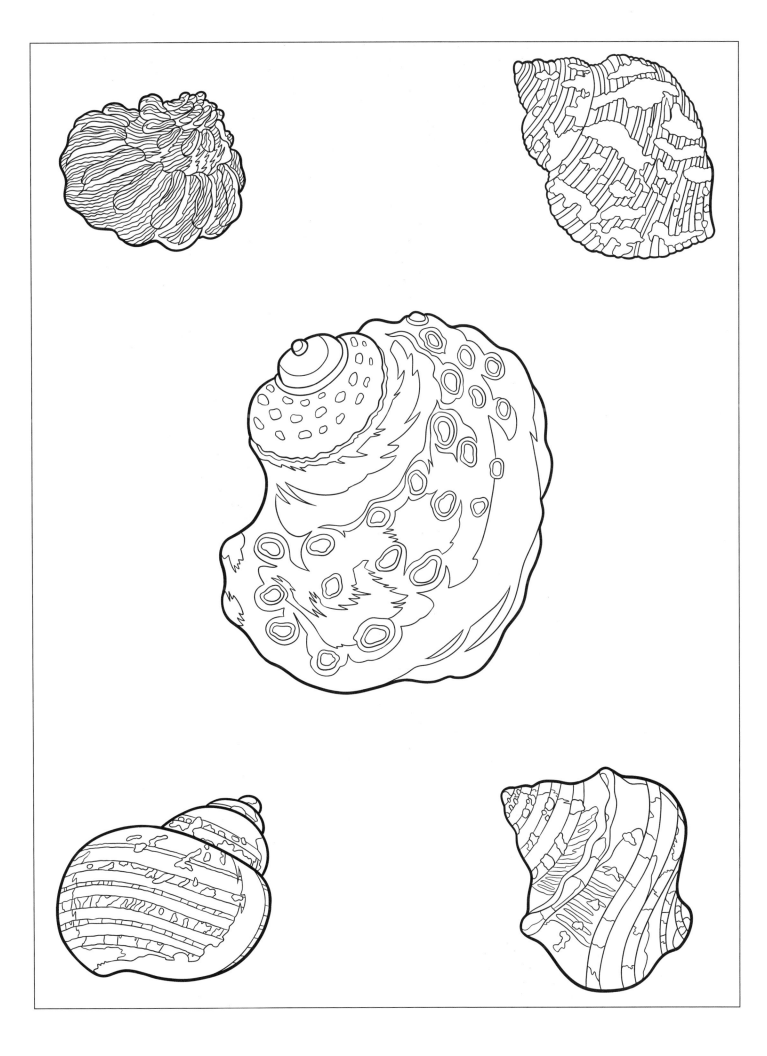

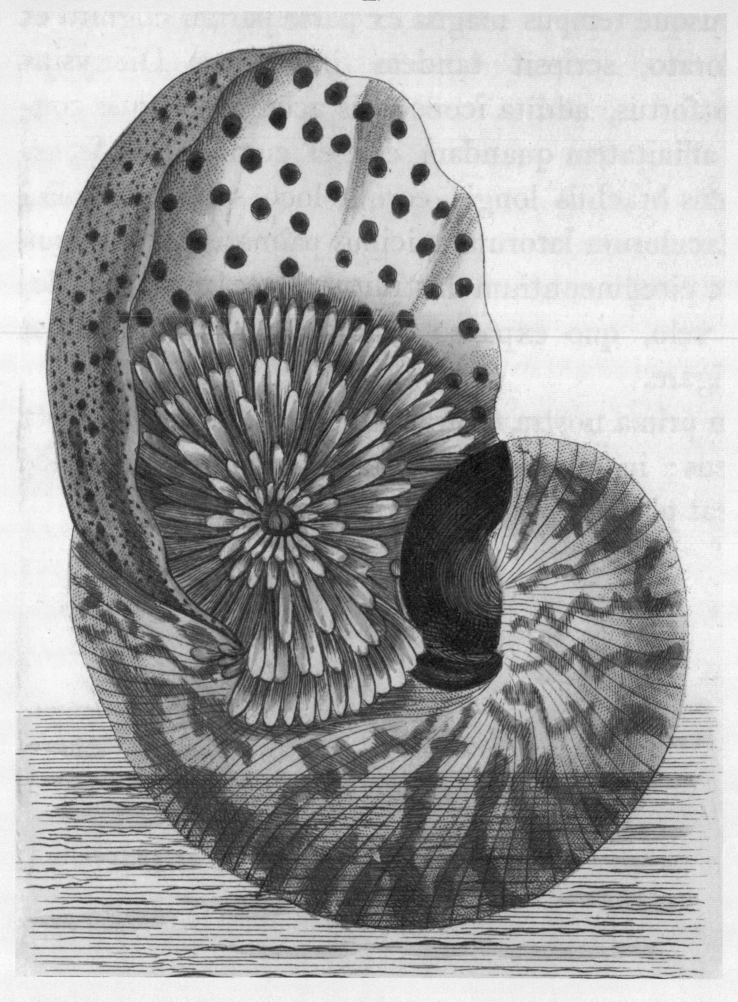

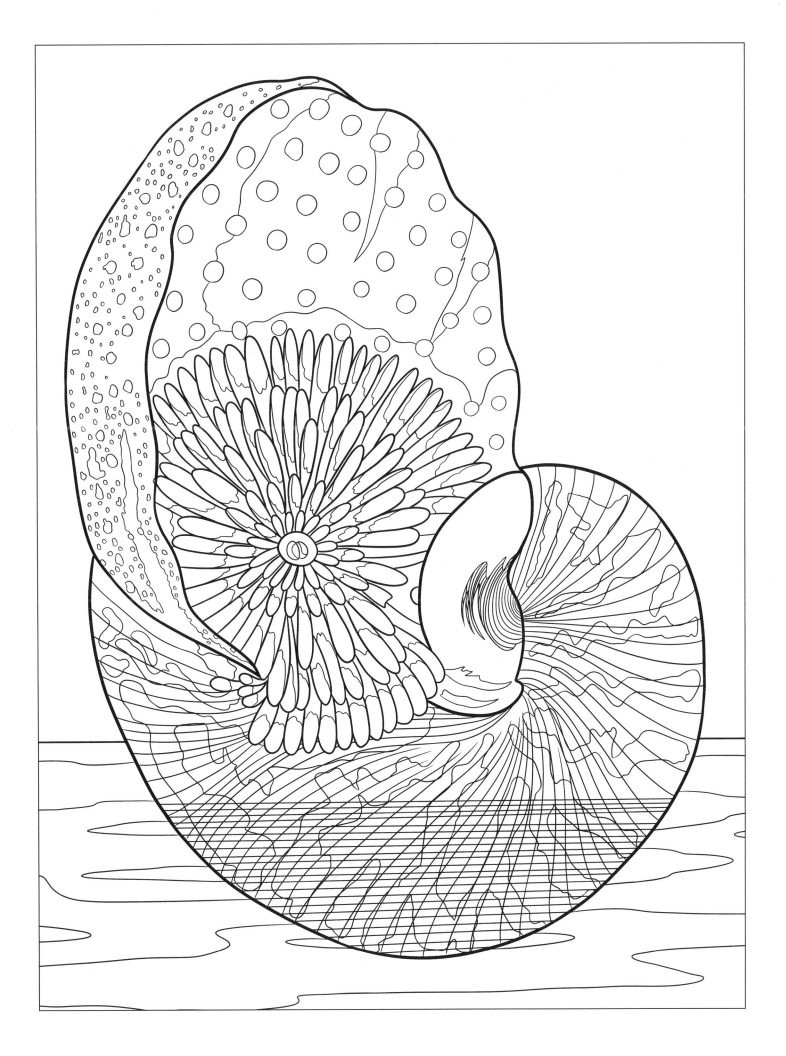

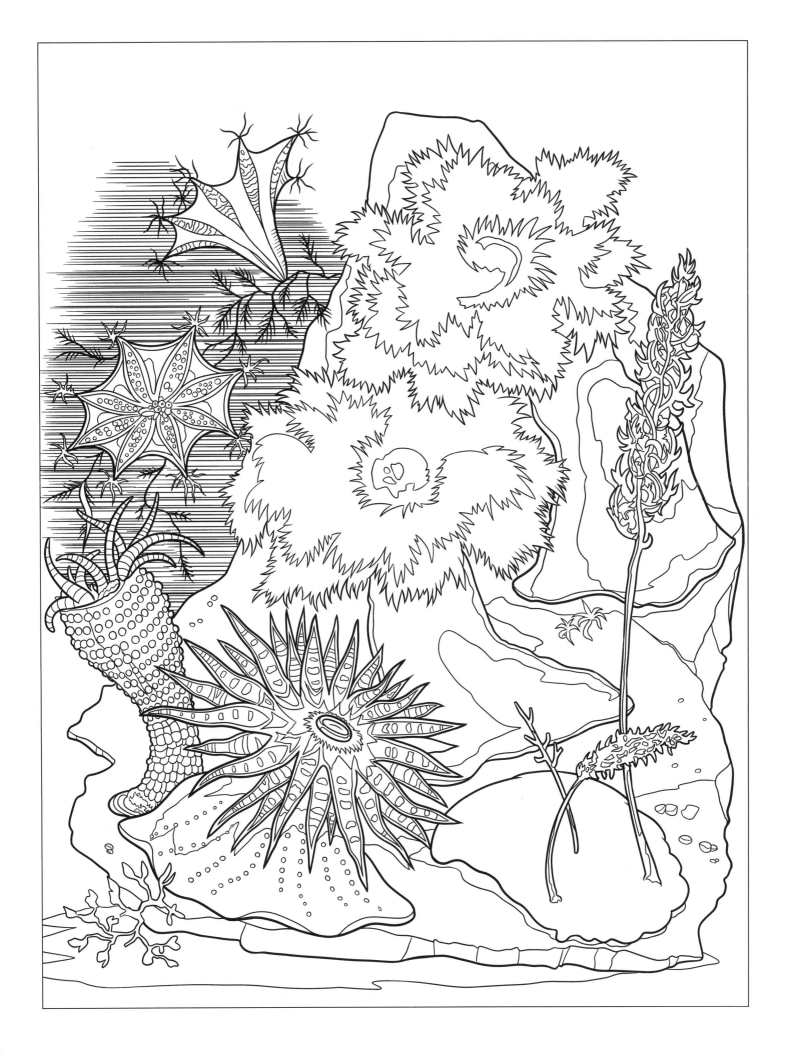

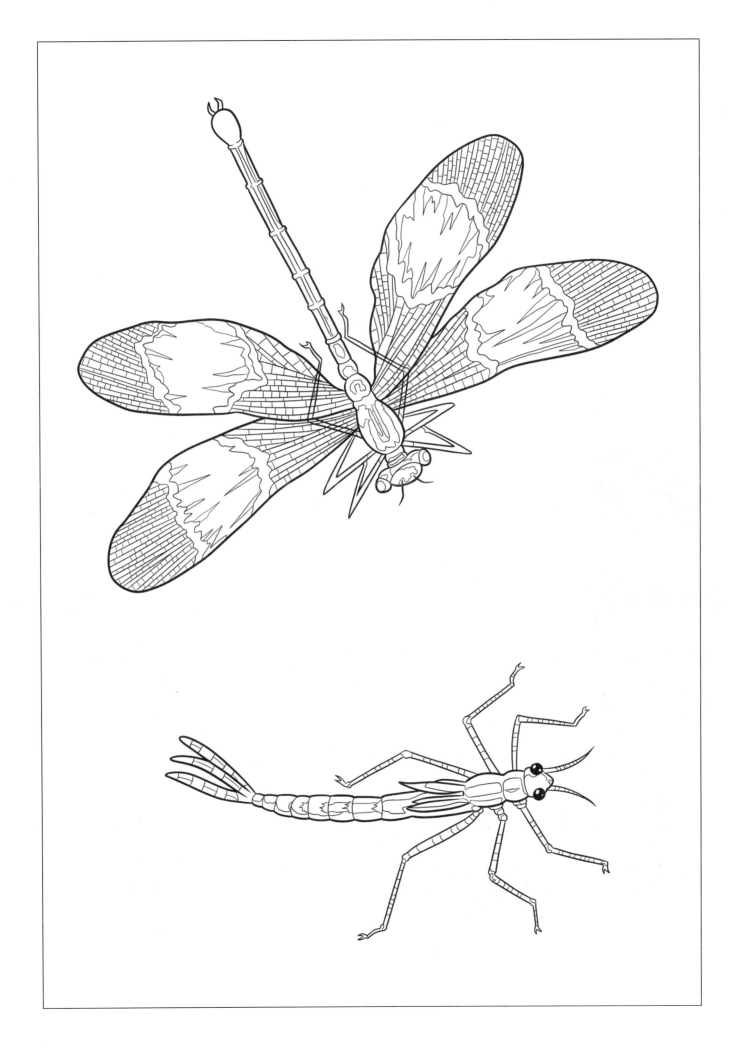

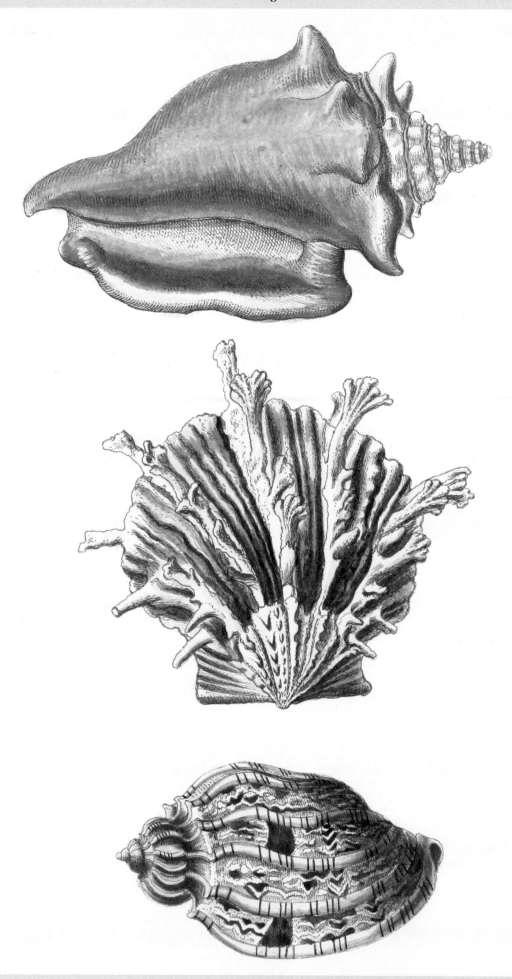

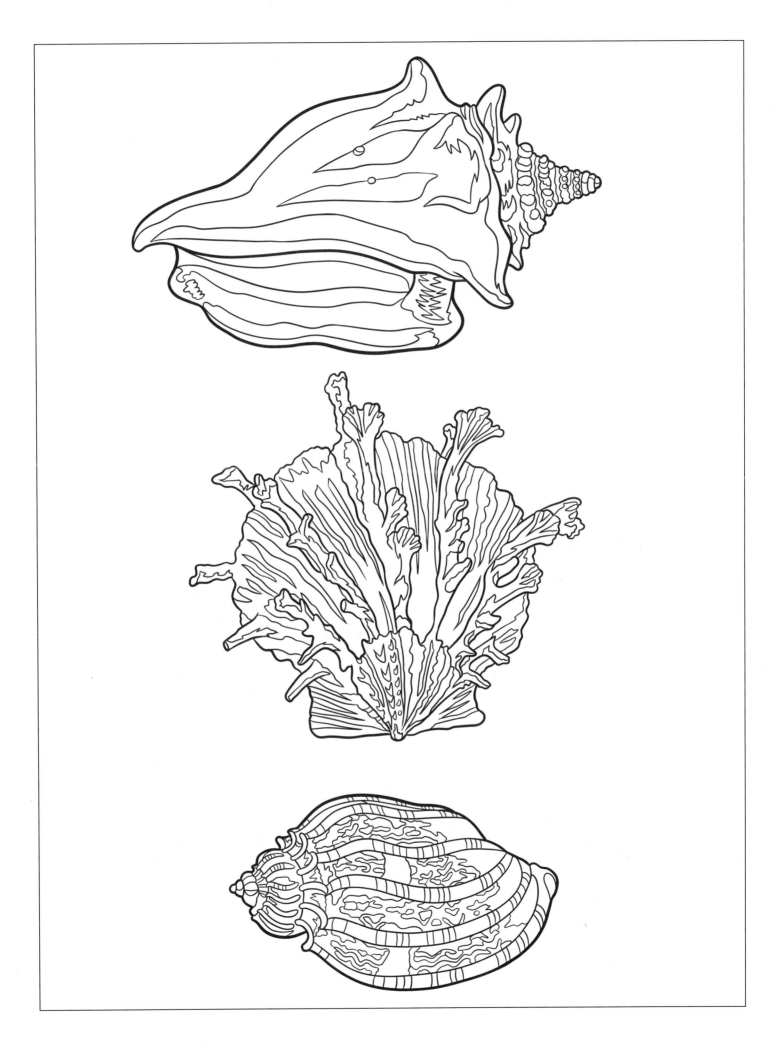

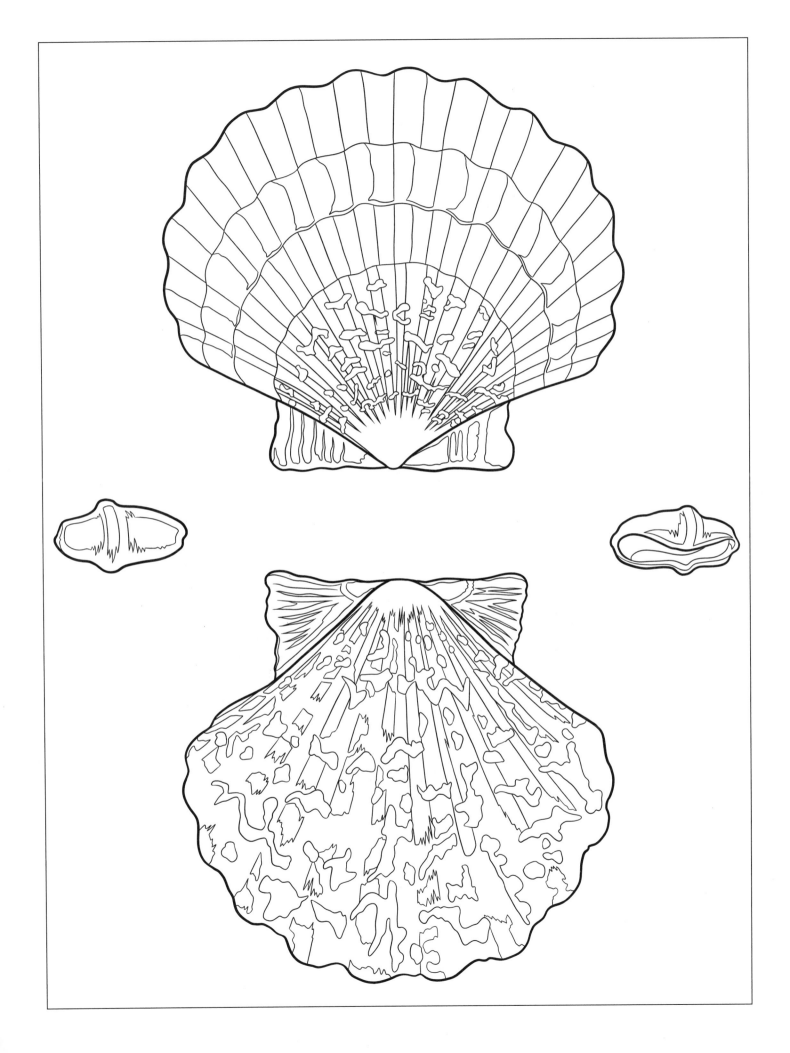

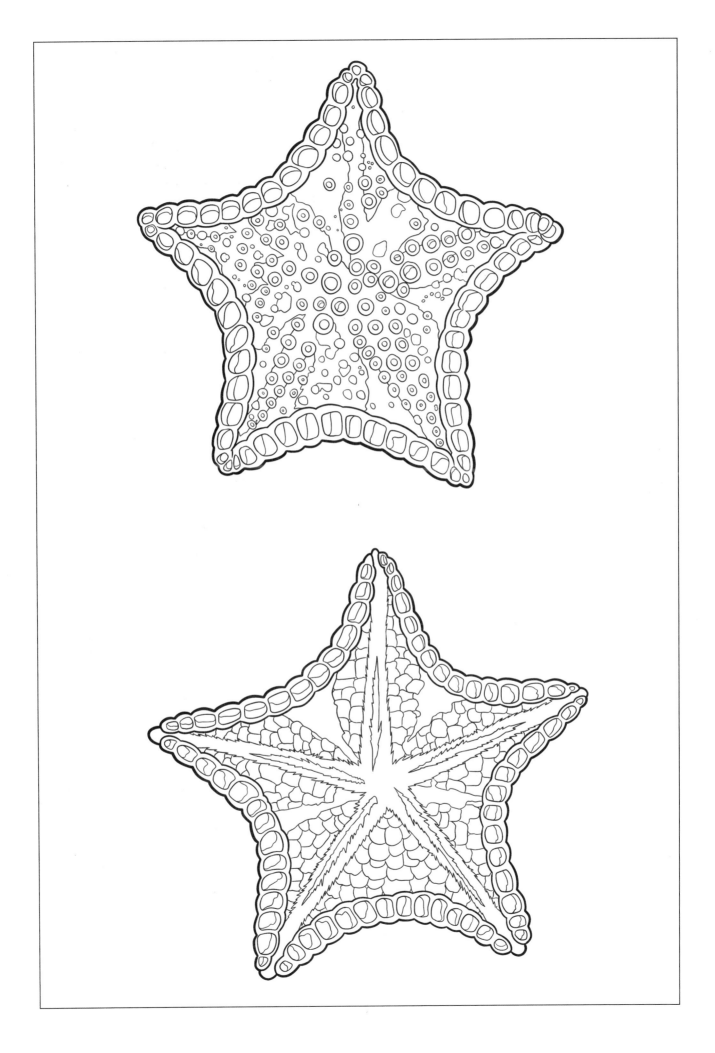

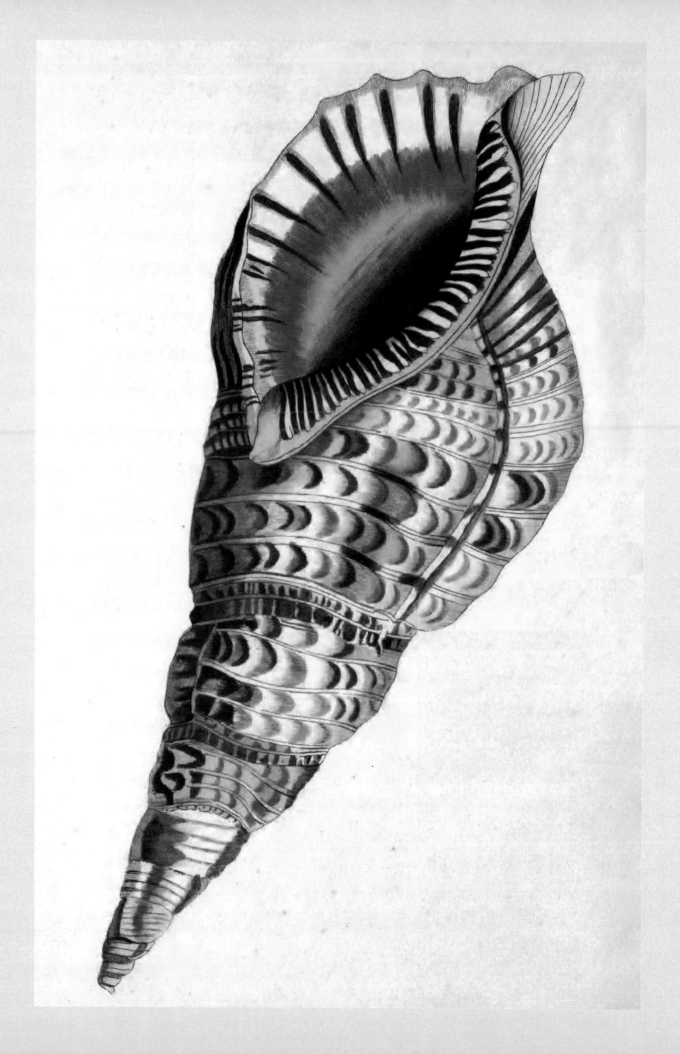

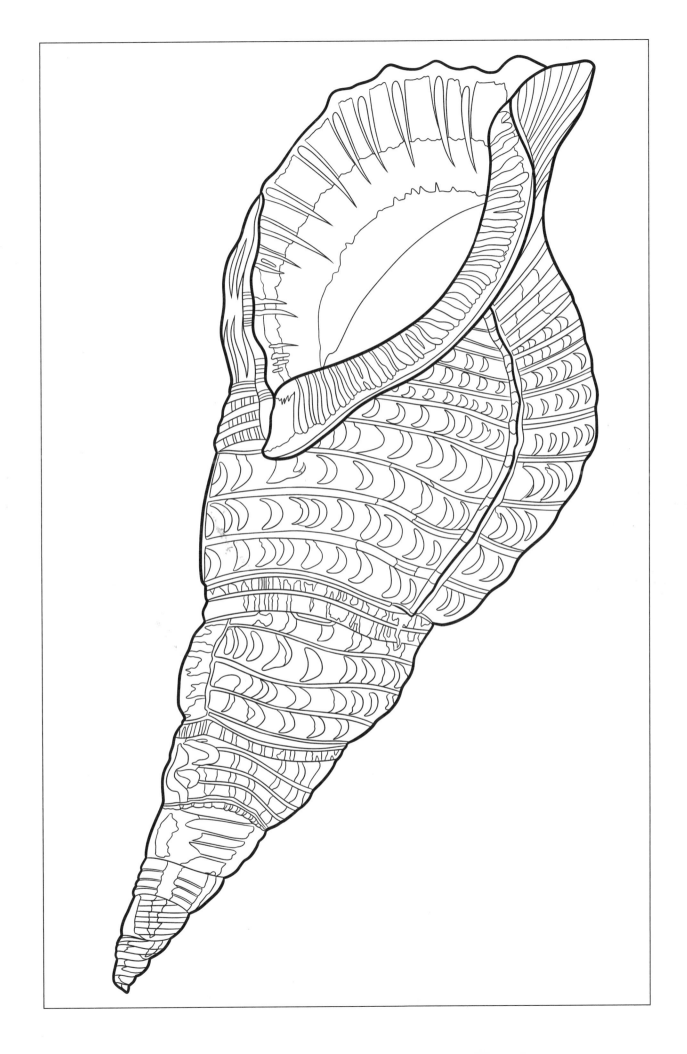